I0440154

Table Of Contents

Chapter 1: Introduction to Independent Contractor Tax Planning

Understanding the Importance of Tax Planning for Independent Contractors

Tax planning is a critical aspect of financial management for independent contractors. As a contractor, you have the flexibility and freedom to work for yourself, but it also means that you have additional responsibilities when it comes to managing your taxes. In this subchapter, we will explore the significance of tax planning for independent contractors and how it can benefit you in various ways.

Tax deductions play a vital role in reducing your overall tax liability. As an independent contractor, you have the advantage of claiming a wide range of deductions that can significantly lower your taxable income. This subchapter will delve into the various tax deductions available to independent contractors, such as home office expenses, business-related travel and meals, professional development costs, and even a portion of your health insurance premiums. By understanding and taking advantage of these deductions, you can maximize your tax savings and keep more money in your pocket.

Effective tax planning is not just about deductions; it also involves strategic decision-making throughout the year. This subchapter will guide you through the essential aspects of tax planning for self-employed individuals. We will explore the importance of accurately estimating and setting aside funds for quarterly tax payments, as well as the significance of maintaining meticulous records of your income and expenses. By staying organized and proactive in your tax planning, you can avoid surprises at tax time and ensure that you are making the most of available deductions.

Navigating the complex IRS guidelines can be daunting, but this subchapter will break it down into easily understandable concepts. We will provide you with an overview of the IRS guidelines for tax planning as a contractor, including the criteria for determining your independent contractor status, the self-employment tax, and the importance of filing your taxes correctly and on time. Understanding these guidelines will enable you to comply with the tax laws and avoid any potential penalties or audits.

In conclusion, tax planning is a crucial aspect of financial management for independent contractors. By understanding the various tax deductions available to you, implementing effective tax planning strategies throughout the year, and staying informed about IRS guidelines, you can optimize your tax savings and ensure compliance with tax laws. This subchapter aims to equip you with the knowledge and tools necessary to navigate the complex world of taxes and make informed decisions that will benefit your financial well-being as an independent contractor.

Overview of the IRS and Its Role in Tax Planning

When it comes to tax planning, independent contractors need to be well-versed in the workings of the Internal Revenue Service (IRS) and its role in the taxation process. Understanding how the IRS operates and the guidelines it sets forth is crucial for contractors who want to maximize tax deductions and effectively plan their finances.

The IRS is the United States federal agency responsible for enforcing and administering the country's tax laws. Its primary role is to collect taxes, ensure compliance with tax laws, and provide assistance to taxpayers. As an independent contractor, it is essential to have a basic understanding of the IRS and its functions to navigate the complexities of tax planning effectively.

What is the IRS? The IRS stands for the Internal Revenue Service. It's a government agency in the United States responsible for collecting taxes and enforcing tax laws. Its primary function is to ensure that individuals and organizations comply with tax laws by paying the correct amount of taxes they owe. The IRS also provides information and assistance to taxpayers, processes tax returns, and investigates cases of tax evasion or fraud. The IRS was created in 1862 during the presidency of Abraham Lincoln. The Revenue Act of 1862 established the position of Commissioner of Internal Revenue and created the Bureau of Internal Revenue, the predecessor to the modern-day IRS.

It was primarily formed to fund the Civil War effort. The federal government needed additional revenue to finance the war, so the income tax system was established as a way to generate funds. Initially, it was a temporary measure, but it laid the groundwork for the income tax system that continues to this day. Over time, the IRS has evolved and expanded its responsibilities beyond collecting taxes for various government programs and functions.

For independent contractors, tax deductions play a vital role in reducing taxable income. This subchapter will delve into the various tax deductions available to contractors and how to leverage them to minimize tax liabilities. It will cover common deductions such as home office expenses, business-related travel, vehicle expenses, and health insurance premiums. By understanding IRS guidelines for tax deductions, contractors can optimize their tax planning strategies and potentially save significant amounts of money.

Tax planning is particularly important for self-employed individuals as they are responsible for paying self-employment taxes. This subchapter will outline effective tax planning strategies for self-employed contractors, including estimated tax payments, retirement contributions, and maximizing deductions. It will provide practical tips and advice to ensure contractors can plan their finances efficiently and avoid any surprises come tax season.

The IRS provides guidelines and resources specifically tailored to independent contractors for tax planning purposes. This subchapter will explore these guidelines and explain how contractors can use them to their advantage. It will cover topics such as recordkeeping, reporting income and expenses, and understanding the different tax forms applicable to contractors. By following IRS guidelines, contractors can ensure compliance with tax laws and make informed decisions to minimize their tax burdens.

In conclusion, this subchapter provides an overview of the IRS and its role in tax planning for independent contractors. By understanding how the IRS operates, contractors can make informed decisions to maximize tax deductions, plan their finances effectively, and ensure compliance with tax laws. With the right knowledge and strategies, contractors can navigate the complexities of the IRS and optimize their tax planning efforts.

Common Mistakes to Avoid as an Independent Contractor

Being an independent contractor comes with a lot of perks, such as the freedom to choose your own projects and set your own schedule. However, it also means you are solely responsible for your taxes and financial planning. To help you navigate the complex world of tax planning as an independent contractor, we have compiled a list of common mistakes to avoid. By avoiding these pitfalls, you can save money and ensure compliance with IRS guidelines.

One of the most significant mistakes that independent contractors make is failing to take advantage of all available tax deductions. As an independent contractor, you are eligible for a wide range of deductions, including business expenses, office supplies, travel costs, and even a portion of your home office expenses. Many contractors overlook these deductions or fail to keep proper records, resulting in missed opportunities to reduce their tax liability.

Another common mistake is not engaging in tax planning throughout the year. Many independent contractors wait until the last minute to gather their financial documents and start thinking about their taxes. By not planning ahead, you may miss out on potential tax-saving opportunities. Instead, consider working with a tax professional who specializes in working with independent contractors. They can help you create a tax plan that maximizes deductions and ensures you are compliant with IRS guidelines.

Failing to separate personal and business expenses is another mistake that independent contractors often make. It is crucial to keep personal and business finances separate to simplify your record-keeping and avoid potential IRS scrutiny. Open a separate bank account for your business income and expenses, and use a dedicated credit card for business-related purchases. By doing so, you can easily track your expenses and ensure accurate reporting when it comes time to file your taxes.

Lastly, many independent contractors neglect to keep meticulous records of their income and expenses. The IRS requires you to keep records for at least three years, and failing to do so can lead to penalties and fines. Invest in accounting software or hire an accountant to help you organize your financial documents and keep track of your income and expenses throughout the year.

In conclusion, as an independent contractor, it is crucial to avoid common mistakes that can lead to unnecessary tax liabilities and potential legal issues. By taking advantage of tax deductions, engaging in year-round tax planning, separating personal and business expenses, and maintaining meticulous records, you can navigate the IRS with confidence and optimize your tax planning strategies. Remember, seeking the guidance of a tax professional who specializes in working with independent contractors can be invaluable in ensuring your financial success as an independent contractor.

Chapter 2: Tax Deductions for Independent Contractors

Identifying Eligible Business Expenses for Independent Contractors

As an independent contractor, understanding which expenses qualify as deductible business expenses is crucial for maximizing your tax savings. By taking advantage of the available deductions, you can significantly reduce your tax liability and keep more of your hard-earned money. In this subchapter, we will explore the key considerations and guidelines for identifying eligible business expenses as an independent contractor.

Tax deductions for independent contractors play a vital role in minimizing your taxable income. These deductions are expenses directly related to your business operations and can be claimed on your tax return. However, it is crucial to ensure that these expenses meet the criteria set by the Internal Revenue Service (IRS). This subchapter will help you navigate the complexities of tax planning for self-employed individuals and ensure your deductions are in compliance with IRS guidelines.

The IRS provides clear guidelines for tax planning as a contractor, and it is essential to familiarize yourself with these rules to avoid any potential penalties or audits. Common eligible business expenses for independent contractors include office supplies, travel expenses, advertising costs, professional memberships, and equipment purchases. Additionally, expenses relating to maintaining a home office, such as rent, utilities, and internet bills, may also qualify for deductions.

To accurately identify eligible business expenses, it is crucial to maintain meticulous records and documentation. This includes keeping receipts, invoices, and any other relevant documentation that supports your claim. It is recommended to use accounting software or tools specifically designed for independent contractors to streamline this process and ensure accuracy.

Furthermore, understanding the difference between personal and business expenses is crucial. While personal expenses are generally not deductible, there may be instances where certain expenses have both personal and business components. In such cases, only the portion directly related to your business operations can be claimed as a deduction.

In conclusion, identifying eligible business expenses is essential for independent contractors to optimize their tax planning strategies. By staying informed about IRS guidelines, maintaining thorough records, and distinguishing between personal and business expenses, you can ensure that you are taking full advantage of available deductions. By doing so, you can minimize your tax liability and maximize your financial success as an independent contractor.

Home Office Deductions and Requirements

As an independent contractor, one of the key aspects of tax planning is understanding the home office deductions and requirements set forth by the IRS. By taking advantage of these deductions, you can significantly reduce your tax liability and maximize your profits. In this subchapter, we will delve into the intricacies of home office deductions and provide you with the necessary guidance to navigate this aspect of tax planning effectively.

The IRS allows independent contractors to deduct expenses related to their home office if it is used exclusively for business purposes. This means that if you have a designated area in your home that is solely used as your workspace, you may be eligible for home office deductions. However, it is crucial to adhere to the IRS guidelines to avoid any potential audit or penalties.

To qualify for home office deductions, your home office must be your principal place of business or a place where you meet clients or customers regularly. It should be used exclusively for conducting business activities and not serve any personal purposes. The IRS also requires that the space be used on a regular basis and be clearly identifiable as a separate area within your home.

Once you meet these requirements, you can deduct a portion of your home-related expenses, including rent or mortgage interest, property taxes, utilities, and insurance. The deduction is calculated based on the square footage of your home office in proportion to the total square footage of your home. This means that if your home office occupies 10% of your home's total square footage, you can deduct 10% of the eligible expenses.

However, it is vital to maintain proper documentation to substantiate your home office deductions. Keep records of all expenses related to your home office, including bills, receipts, and lease agreements. Additionally, maintain a floor plan or photographs that clearly depict the space used as your home office.

Navigating the complexities of home office deductions can be challenging, but with careful planning and adherence to IRS guidelines, you can optimize your tax savings. Consult with a tax professional who specializes in working with independent contractors to ensure you maximize your deductions while staying compliant with the IRS regulations. By taking advantage of home office deductions, you can significantly reduce your tax burden and allocate those savings towards growing your business.

Vehicle and Travel Expenses for Independent Contractors

As an independent contractor, it is essential to understand the various tax deductions and guidelines related to your business expenses. One such area that often confuses contractors is vehicle and travel expenses. In this subchapter, we will explore the tax planning strategies and IRS guidelines specifically tailored for independent contractors regarding their vehicle and travel expenses.

First and foremost, it is important to keep detailed records of all your vehicle expenses. This includes not only the cost of purchasing or leasing the vehicle but also maintenance, repairs, fuel, insurance, and even parking fees. These expenses can be deductible if they are directly related to your business activities. However, it is crucial to differentiate between personal and business use and only claim the portion that is attributable to your self-employment.

To calculate the deductible portion of your vehicle expenses, there are two primary methods: the actual expenses method and the standard mileage rate method. The actual expenses method allows you to deduct the actual costs incurred for your vehicle, whereas the standard mileage rate method offers a fixed rate per mile driven for business purposes. You can choose the method that suits your situation best, but once you select a method, you must stick with it throughout the lifespan of the vehicle.

When it comes to travel expenses, independent contractors often find themselves in situations where they need to travel for business purposes, whether it's attending conferences, meeting clients, or visiting job sites. These expenses can be deductible as well. However, it is crucial to ensure that the travel is necessary and directly related to your self-employment activities. Deductible travel expenses typically include airfare, lodging, meals, and even transportation costs while at your destination.

To avoid any potential issues with the IRS, it is crucial to maintain proper documentation for all your vehicle and travel expenses. Keep track of receipts, invoices, and any other relevant documents to substantiate your deductions. Additionally, it is advisable to consult a tax professional who specializes in working with independent contractors to ensure you are maximizing your deductions while remaining compliant with IRS guidelines.

In conclusion, understanding the tax deductions and guidelines related to vehicle and travel expenses is crucial for independent contractors. By keeping detailed records, choosing the appropriate method for calculating deductions, and maintaining proper documentation, you can navigate the IRS requirements effectively. Remember, tax planning is an essential aspect of being a self-employed individual, and by staying informed, you can ensure optimal financial management and maximize your tax savings.

Health Insurance and Retirement Contributions

As an independent contractor, understanding the intricacies of tax planning is crucial to maximizing your financial well-being. Two key areas that require careful consideration are health insurance and retirement contributions. This subchapter will guide you through the essential aspects of these topics, providing valuable insights and strategies to help you navigate the IRS requirements and optimize your tax planning.

Health insurance is a vital aspect of everyone's life, and as a contractor, you must take charge of your own coverage. Fortunately, the IRS provides tax deductions for independent contractors to help offset the costs. This means that you can deduct the premiums you pay for health insurance, including coverage for yourself, your spouse, and dependents, from your taxable income. However, there are certain criteria that must be met to qualify for these deductions. This subchapter will outline these criteria and provide tips on how to ensure your health insurance deductions are properly claimed.

In addition to health insurance, retirement planning is an equally important consideration for independent contractors. While traditional employees often have access to employer-sponsored retirement plans, contractors must take individual responsibility for their retirement savings. The good news is that the IRS offers various retirement contribution options that can provide tax advantages to self-employed individuals. This subchapter will delve into these options, including simplified employee pension (SEP) IRAs, solo 401(k) plans, and individual retirement accounts (IRAs). By understanding the nuances of these retirement vehicles, you can make informed decisions about contributing to your retirement while simultaneously optimizing your tax planning.

To ensure compliance with IRS guidelines, it's essential to understand the specific rules and regulations that pertain to tax planning as a contractor. This subchapter will provide an overview of the IRS guidelines pertaining to tax deductions for independent contractors, tax planning for self-employed individuals, and other relevant regulations.

By staying informed and up-to-date on these guidelines, you can avoid potential pitfalls and maximize your tax planning strategies.

In conclusion, health insurance and retirement contributions are critical components of tax planning for independent contractors. By leveraging the available tax deductions for health insurance and exploring the various retirement contribution options, contractors can optimize their financial well-being while maintaining compliance with IRS guidelines. This subchapter aims to equip you with the necessary knowledge and strategies to navigate these aspects successfully, allowing you to make informed decisions and achieve your financial goals as an independent contractor.

Maximizing Deductions for Materials, Supplies, and Equipment

As an independent contractor, understanding and utilizing tax deductions can significantly impact your bottom line. One area where contractors often overlook potential deductions is in the category of materials, supplies, and equipment. By maximizing deductions in this area, you can effectively reduce your taxable income, increasing your overall profitability.

When it comes to materials, supplies, and equipment, the IRS allows contractors to deduct the expenses incurred in purchasing and using these items for their business operations. This includes everything from the cost of raw materials to the tools and equipment necessary to complete your projects. By keeping thorough records and understanding the specific guidelines set forth by the IRS, you can ensure that you are taking full advantage of these deductions.

To maximize your deductions for materials, supplies, and equipment, it is essential to categorize and track your expenses properly. The IRS requires contractors to differentiate between materials and supplies that are consumed directly in the construction process and those that are used to maintain and repair equipment. By accurately classifying your expenses, you can ensure that you are claiming the appropriate deductions for each category.

In addition to categorizing your expenses correctly, it is crucial to keep detailed records of all purchases related to materials, supplies, and equipment. This includes receipts, invoices, and any other documentation that proves the legitimacy of your expenses. By maintaining organized records, you can easily substantiate your deductions if audited by the IRS.

Furthermore, it is important to stay up to date with any changes or updates to the IRS guidelines for tax planning as a contractor. The tax code is constantly evolving, and new regulations may impact the deductions you can claim. By staying informed and consulting with a tax professional, you can ensure that you are taking advantage of all available deductions within the boundaries of the law.

In conclusion, maximizing deductions for materials, supplies, and equipment is a critical aspect of tax planning for independent contractors. By properly categorizing and documenting your expenses, as well as staying informed about IRS guidelines, you can reduce your taxable income and increase your profitability. Remember, consulting with a tax professional is always advisable to ensure compliance and optimize your tax planning strategies.

Deductions for Advertising and Marketing Expenses

As an independent contractor, one of the key aspects of running your own business is ensuring that you effectively market your services to potential clients. Luckily, the Internal Revenue Service (IRS) recognizes the importance of advertising and marketing for contractors and allows you to deduct these expenses from your taxable income. Understanding the deductions available for advertising and marketing expenses can significantly reduce your tax liability and improve your overall financial position.

Advertising and marketing expenses include a wide range of activities aimed at promoting your services, such as website development, online advertisements, print media, trade show participation, and even business cards. These expenses are considered ordinary and necessary for your business and are therefore eligible for deductions.

When deducting advertising and marketing expenses, it is important to keep accurate records of all your expenditures. This includes keeping receipts, invoices, and any other documentation that proves the nature and purpose of the expenses incurred. By maintaining meticulous records, you can easily substantiate your deductions in case of an IRS audit.

The IRS allows you to deduct the full cost of advertising and marketing expenses that directly relate to your business. However, it is crucial to distinguish between expenses that are solely for advertising and marketing purposes and those that may have a personal component. For example, if you combine business and personal expenses on a single platform, such as a website, you can only deduct the portion directly related to your business.

Additionally, the IRS may require you to determine the period of time over which you can deduct certain advertising and marketing expenses. Some expenses, such as website development costs, may need to be amortized over a specific period rather than deducted in a single year.

Proper tax planning for independent contractors involves staying informed about the current IRS guidelines and regulations. By understanding the deductibility of advertising and marketing expenses, you can strategically plan your budget and maximize your deductions to minimize your tax liability.

In conclusion, as an independent contractor, it is important to take advantage of the deductions available for advertising and marketing expenses. By keeping accurate records, distinguishing between personal and business expenses, and staying informed about IRS guidelines, you can effectively reduce your tax liability and improve your overall financial success. Remember, tax planning is an essential part of managing your business, and understanding the deductions for advertising and marketing expenses is a valuable tool in your tax planning strategy.

Chapter 3: Tax Planning Strategies for Self-Employed Individuals

Choosing the Right Business Structure for Tax Advantages

When it comes to tax planning strategies for independent contractors, one of the most crucial decisions you will have to make is choosing the right business structure. The business structure you select can have significant implications on your tax liabilities, deductions, and overall financial success. Understanding the various options available to you and their corresponding tax advantages is essential in navigating the complex world of tax planning as a contractor.

There are several business structures you can consider as an independent contractor, each with its unique tax implications. The most common options include sole proprietorship, partnership, limited liability company (LLC), and S corporation. Let's explore each of these structures and the tax advantages they offer.

Sole proprietorship is the simplest and most common business structure for independent contractors. It provides complete control and flexibility over your business operations. However, as a sole proprietor, you are personally liable for all business debts and obligations. From a tax perspective, sole proprietors report their business income and expenses on Schedule C of their personal tax return. This structure allows contractors to take advantage of various tax deductions, such as home office expenses, travel expenses, and equipment purchases.

Partnerships are another option if you collaborate with other contractors or professionals. In a partnership, each partner contributes to the business's daily operations and shares in the profits and losses. From a tax standpoint, partnerships file an informational return (Form 1065), but the income and deductions pass through to the individual partners' personal tax returns. This structure allows for increased tax flexibility and allows partners to deduct their share of business expenses.

Limited liability companies (LLCs) combine the liability protection of a corporation with the flexibility and tax advantages of a partnership or sole proprietorship. As an independent contractor, forming an LLC can help shield your personal assets from business liabilities. From a tax perspective, LLCs have the option to be treated as a disregarded entity (sole proprietorship), partnership, or even an S corporation, depending on the number of members and their preferences.

S corporations are a popular choice for independent contractors looking to minimize self-employment taxes. By electing S corporation status, you can potentially reduce the portion of income subject to self-employment tax. S corporations file a separate tax return, and shareholders report their share of income and losses on their individual tax returns.

Choosing the right business structure for tax advantages requires careful consideration of your specific circumstances and goals. It is crucial to consult with a qualified tax professional who can guide you through the decision-making process and help you maximize your tax benefits as an independent contractor.

In conclusion, understanding the different business structures available and their corresponding tax advantages is essential for independent contractors. By selecting the appropriate structure, contractors can optimize their tax planning strategies, maximize deductions, and ultimately achieve financial success. So, take the time to evaluate your options, seek professional advice, and make an informed decision that aligns with your business goals and tax planning objectives.

Understanding Estimated Tax Payments and Avoiding Penalties

As an independent contractor, understanding estimated tax payments is crucial for managing your tax obligations and avoiding potential penalties from the Internal Revenue Service (IRS). This subchapter aims to provide you with a comprehensive overview of estimated tax payments, along with practical strategies to help you navigate the complex tax landscape.

Estimated tax payments refer to the method by which self-employed individuals, like contractors, pay their taxes throughout the year. Unlike traditional employees who have taxes automatically withheld from their paychecks, contractors are responsible for calculating and paying their taxes directly to the IRS. Failure to make these payments can lead to penalties and interest charges, making it essential to stay on top of your estimated tax obligations.

The first step in understanding estimated tax payments is to determine whether you are required to make them. Generally, if you expect to owe at least $1,000 in taxes after subtracting any tax credits and withholding, you are obligated to make quarterly estimated tax payments. However, certain exceptions may apply, and it is crucial to consult the IRS guidelines to determine your specific obligations.

To avoid penalties, careful tax planning is essential. Start by accurately estimating your income for the year, taking into consideration any fluctuations or seasonal variations that may impact your earnings. By projecting your income, you can calculate your estimated tax liability and divide it into four equal payments to be made throughout the year. This approach ensures you meet your tax obligations without facing the burden of a large lump-sum payment at tax time.

Additionally, exploring tax deductions specific to independent contractors can significantly reduce your tax liability. Deductions such as home office expenses, business-related travel, and professional development costs can help offset your taxable income, ultimately reducing the amount you owe in taxes. By understanding the available deductions and keeping detailed records, you can maximize your tax savings and optimize your financial situation.

In conclusion, understanding estimated tax payments and implementing effective tax planning strategies are crucial for independent contractors. By accurately estimating your income, making timely estimated tax payments, and taking advantage of applicable tax deductions, you can navigate the IRS guidelines with confidence and avoid penalties. Stay informed, consult with tax professionals when necessary, and proactively manage your tax obligations to ensure financial success as an independent contractor.

Utilizing Retirement Plans for Tax Savings

As an independent contractor, it is essential to take advantage of every opportunity to save on taxes and maximize your income. One effective strategy to achieve this is by utilizing retirement plans. Retirement plans not only help secure your financial future but also offer significant tax benefits that can enhance your overall tax planning strategy. In this subchapter, we will explore how contractors can utilize retirement plans to minimize their tax liability and optimize their savings.

Tax deductions for independent contractors can be a valuable tool to reduce taxable income. By contributing to retirement plans, such as traditional IRAs, Simplified Employee Pension (SEP) IRAs, or solo 401(k)s, contractors can deduct their contributions from their income, thereby lowering their overall tax liability. These deductions not only reduce the amount of taxes owed but also allow contractors to save more money for retirement.

Tax planning for self-employed individuals requires careful consideration of retirement plan options. Traditional IRAs, SEP IRAs, and solo 401(k)s are popular choices among contractors. Traditional IRAs offer tax-deferred growth, allowing contributions to grow tax-free until withdrawals are made during retirement. SEP IRAs are ideal for contractors with no employees, as they allow for higher contribution limits. Solo 401(k)s provide even greater flexibility, allowing for higher contribution limits and the potential for loans.

The IRS guidelines for tax planning as a contractor are specific and understanding them is crucial. Contractors must ensure they are contributing within the limits set by the IRS to avoid penalties or potential audits. Additionally, contractors should stay informed about any changes to retirement plan rules and regulations to make informed decisions about their tax planning strategies.

By utilizing retirement plans, contractors can not only reduce their current tax liability but also build a strong foundation for their future financial security. By taking advantage of the various retirement plan options available, contractors can tailor their tax planning strategy to their unique needs and goals. Working closely with a financial advisor or tax professional can help contractors navigate the complexities of retirement planning and ensure they are maximizing their tax savings.

In conclusion, retirement plans offer independent contractors valuable tax benefits, allowing them to reduce their taxable income and save for retirement. By understanding the available retirement plan options, contractors can make informed decisions that align with their tax planning strategies. It is essential to stay updated on IRS guidelines and seek professional advice to ensure compliance and optimize tax savings. By utilizing retirement plans effectively, contractors can secure a financially stable future while minimizing their tax liability.

Leveraging Tax Credits for Self-Employed Individuals

As an independent contractor, understanding tax planning strategies is crucial for maximizing your financial benefits. One powerful tool at your disposal is leveraging tax credits. This subchapter will delve into the various tax credits available to self-employed individuals, providing you with valuable insights on how to reduce your tax liability and optimize your financial situation.

Tax credits can significantly impact your tax return by directly reducing the amount of tax you owe. Unlike deductions, which subtract a portion of your income before calculating taxes, tax credits directly decrease the amount of tax owed after it has been calculated. This makes tax credits an attractive option for contractors looking to maximize their tax savings.

There are several tax credits specifically designed for self-employed individuals. One such credit is the Earned Income Tax Credit (EITC). Available to low to moderate-income individuals, the EITC can provide a substantial refund and is particularly beneficial for contractors with dependents. By understanding the eligibility criteria and taking advantage of this credit, you can potentially receive a significant tax refund.

Another valuable tax credit is the Child and Dependent Care Credit. If you incur expenses for childcare while working as an independent contractor, you may be eligible for this credit. This credit can help offset a significant portion of your childcare expenses, allowing you to save a substantial amount of money.

Additionally, the Health Coverage Tax Credit (HCTC) is an essential credit to consider. As a self-employed individual, finding affordable health insurance can be challenging. The HCTC provides a tax credit to help cover the cost of health insurance premiums, making it easier for contractors to access quality healthcare coverage.

Navigating the IRS guidelines for tax planning as a contractor is crucial to ensure you qualify for and make the most of these tax credits. Staying up-to-date with the latest regulations and understanding the eligibility requirements will empower you to leverage these credits effectively.

In conclusion, understanding and leveraging tax credits is a crucial aspect of tax planning for self-employed individuals. By familiarizing yourself with the various tax credits available to contractors and ensuring compliance with IRS guidelines, you can significantly reduce your tax liability and optimize your financial situation. Take advantage of these valuable tax credits and maximize your tax savings as an independent contractor.

Managing Cash Flow and Tax Liability throughout the Year

As an independent contractor, understanding how to manage your cash flow and tax liability throughout the year is crucial for your financial success. By effectively planning and strategizing your tax deductions, you can minimize your tax burden and maximize your profits. This subchapter aims to provide you with valuable insights and guidelines on managing cash flow and tax liability, ensuring you stay compliant with IRS regulations while optimizing your financial situation.

One of the key aspects of managing cash flow is to keep track of your income and expenses meticulously. Maintaining accurate records of all your business transactions allows you to determine your taxable income accurately. By utilizing bookkeeping software or hiring a professional accountant, you can streamline this process and ensure you have a clear picture of your financial situation.

Understanding tax deductions specific to independent contractors is another crucial aspect of managing your tax liability. By familiarizing yourself with the IRS guidelines for tax planning as a contractor, you can identify deductible expenses and reduce your taxable income. This includes deductions for home office expenses, travel and transportation costs, professional development, equipment and supplies, and health insurance premiums, among others. By leveraging these deductions effectively, you can significantly lower your overall tax liability.

Tax planning for self-employed individuals requires a proactive approach. Instead of waiting until the end of the year to address your tax obligations, it is advisable to plan throughout the year. Regularly review your financial situation and consult with a tax professional to identify potential tax-saving opportunities. By estimating your tax liability periodically, you can make estimated tax payments to avoid penalties and ensure a smooth cash flow.

Additionally, it is essential to stay up to date with any changes in tax laws and regulations. The IRS frequently updates its guidelines, and being aware of these changes can help you make informed decisions regarding your tax planning strategies. Consider attending seminars or workshops that focus on tax planning for independent contractors to stay informed and gain valuable insights from experts in the field.

In conclusion, effectively managing cash flow and tax liability is crucial for the financial success of independent contractors. By understanding tax deductions, planning throughout the year, and staying informed about IRS guidelines, you can optimize your tax situation and ensure compliance with tax regulations. Implementing sound financial practices and seeking professional advice when needed will empower you to navigate the complex world of taxes and achieve long-term financial stability.

Working with a Tax Professional to Optimize Tax Planning

Tax planning can be a complex and daunting task for independent contractors. With constantly changing tax laws and regulations, it is crucial to have a solid understanding of how to optimize your tax planning strategies. One way to ease this burden and ensure you are maximizing your tax deductions is by working with a tax professional.

Tax professionals are experts in navigating the intricate world of tax planning. They have a deep understanding of the IRS guidelines and can provide valuable advice tailored to your specific situation. By partnering with a tax professional, you can gain peace of mind knowing that your tax planning is in capable hands.

One of the key benefits of working with a tax professional is their ability to identify all eligible tax deductions for independent contractors. As an independent contractor, you are entitled to deduct a wide range of expenses related to your business. However, it can be challenging to determine which expenses are deductible and how to properly document them. A tax professional can guide you through this process, ensuring you are taking advantage of every possible deduction and minimizing your tax liability.

Tax planning for self-employed individuals requires careful consideration of various factors. A tax professional can help you devise a comprehensive tax strategy that takes into account your business structure, income sources, and future goals. They can advise you on the most tax-efficient ways to structure your business and manage your finances. This includes recommending whether to operate as a sole proprietorship, partnership, or corporation, and helping you understand the tax implications of each option.

IRS guidelines for tax planning as a contractor can sometimes be complex and confusing. A tax professional can help you navigate these guidelines, ensuring you are in compliance with all applicable laws and regulations. They can assist you in understanding the self-employment tax, estimated tax payments, and other tax obligations specific to independent contractors.

In conclusion, working with a tax professional can greatly optimize your tax planning as an independent contractor. Their expertise and knowledge of tax laws and regulations will help you identify all eligible deductions, develop a comprehensive tax strategy, and ensure compliance with IRS guidelines. By partnering with a tax professional, you can minimize your tax liability and focus on what you do best – running your business.

Chapter 4: IRS Guidelines for Tax Planning as a Contractor

Reporting Income and Filing Requirements for Independent Contractors

As an independent contractor, it is crucial to understand the reporting income and filing requirements set forth by the IRS. Navigating the complex world of taxes can be overwhelming, but with the right knowledge and strategies, you can maximize your tax deductions and effectively plan your finances. In this subchapter, we will explore the essential guidelines for reporting income and filing requirements specifically tailored for independent contractors.

When it comes to reporting income, independent contractors must be diligent in accurately documenting and reporting all earnings. Unlike regular employees who receive a W-2 form, independent contractors receive a Form 1099-MISC, which details their total income from each client or employer. It is crucial to ensure that all income is accurately reported on your tax return, as failure to do so can result in penalties and audits.

Moreover, independent contractors have the advantage of claiming various tax deductions to reduce their taxable income. This book will delve into the specific tax deductions available to independent contractors, such as home office expenses, travel and transportation costs, professional development expenses, and more. By understanding which deductions apply to your business, you can effectively minimize your tax liability and maximize your financial gains.

Tax planning is another crucial aspect for self-employed individuals. By implementing effective tax planning strategies, you can optimize your finances and take advantage of legal ways to reduce your tax burden. This book will provide you with valuable insights into tax planning techniques that are specifically tailored to contractors, allowing you to make informed decisions and minimize your tax liability throughout the year.

Additionally, this subchapter will explore the IRS guidelines for tax planning as a contractor. It will provide you with a comprehensive understanding of the rules and regulations set forth by the IRS, ensuring that you stay compliant and avoid any potential penalties or audits. By adhering to these guidelines, you can confidently navigate the tax landscape and focus on growing your business.

In conclusion, reporting income and filing requirements for independent contractors is a critical aspect of managing your finances effectively. By understanding the specific guidelines for reporting income, maximizing tax deductions, and implementing sound tax planning strategies, you can optimize your finances and ensure compliance with IRS regulations. This subchapter will equip you with the knowledge and tools necessary to navigate the IRS and confidently plan your taxes as an independent contractor.

Understanding Self-Employment Taxes and Estimated Tax Payments

As an independent contractor, it is crucial to have a solid understanding of self-employment taxes and estimated tax payments. Navigating the complex world of taxes can be overwhelming, but with the right knowledge and strategies, you can effectively plan your tax obligations and maximize your deductions. This subchapter aims to provide contractors with comprehensive information on self-employment taxes, estimated tax payments, and IRS guidelines for tax planning.

Self-employment taxes are essentially the equivalent of Social Security and Medicare taxes for individuals who work for themselves. Unlike traditional employees, you are responsible for paying both the employer and employee portions of these taxes. This means that as a self-employed individual, you must pay a higher percentage of your income in taxes. Understanding the calculation and the impact on your overall tax liability is crucial for effective tax planning.

Estimated tax payments are a way for self-employed individuals to pay their taxes throughout the year, rather than in one lump sum at tax time. These payments are made quarterly and are based on your projected annual income. By paying estimated taxes, you can avoid penalties and interest charges for underpayment. It is important to accurately estimate your income and make timely payments to stay in compliance with IRS regulations.

Tax deductions are an essential part of tax planning for independent contractors. Knowing what expenses you can deduct can significantly reduce your taxable income. This subchapter will explore common deductions available to contractors, such as home office expenses, business-related travel, equipment purchases, and professional development costs. By taking advantage of these deductions, you can minimize your tax liability and keep more of your hard-earned money.

In addition to tax deductions, understanding IRS guidelines for tax planning as a contractor is vital. The IRS has specific rules and regulations for self-employed individuals, and failure to comply with these guidelines can lead to penalties and audits. This subchapter will delve into important topics such as recordkeeping, quarterly tax reporting, and proper classification of workers. By staying informed and following IRS guidelines, you can ensure smooth tax planning and avoid any unnecessary complications.

In conclusion, mastering the concepts of self-employment taxes and estimated tax payments is crucial for independent contractors. By understanding the calculation, making timely estimated tax payments, maximizing deductions, and adhering to IRS guidelines, you can effectively manage your tax obligations and optimize your financial situation. With the knowledge gained from this subchapter, you will be better equipped to navigate the complexities of the tax system and make informed decisions that benefit your business.

Keeping Accurate Records and Documentation for Tax Purposes

As an independent contractor, one of the most crucial aspects of managing your finances and ensuring compliance with the Internal Revenue Service (IRS) is maintaining accurate records and documentation for tax purposes. By doing so, you not only stay organized but also maximize your tax deductions, plan effectively, and adhere to IRS guidelines for tax planning as a contractor. This subchapter will guide you through the essential practices and strategies to help you navigate the complex world of tax planning as an independent contractor.

Accurate record-keeping begins with maintaining a separate business bank account. This will allow you to clearly segregate your business and personal expenses, making it easier to track your income and expenses effectively. Furthermore, it is essential to retain all relevant receipts, invoices, and financial statements. These documents serve as evidence to support your deductions and ensure you can substantiate your claims in case of an audit.

To optimize tax deductions for independent contractors, it is crucial to understand which expenses are deductible. Common deductible expenses include office supplies, travel expenses, professional memberships, and home office expenses, among others. By keeping detailed records of these expenses, you can reduce your taxable income and potentially lower your overall tax liability.

Additionally, accurate documentation is necessary for tax planning purposes. By analyzing your income and expenses throughout the year, you can make informed decisions that will positively impact your tax situation. For instance, if you anticipate a significant increase in income, you may want to consider making estimated tax payments to avoid penalties and interest charges.

IRS guidelines for tax planning as a contractor are constantly evolving. It is crucial to stay updated with the latest regulations and changes to ensure compliance. By maintaining accurate records, you can easily adapt to any modifications in tax laws and regulations and make necessary adjustments to your tax planning strategies.

In conclusion, keeping accurate records and documentation for tax purposes is an integral part of tax planning for self-employed individuals. By implementing effective record-keeping practices, you can maximize your tax deductions, plan strategically, and adhere to IRS guidelines. Remember, staying organized and maintaining detailed records will not only save you time and effort but also provide you with peace of mind knowing that you are in full compliance with the IRS.

Responding to IRS Audits and Inquiries as an Independent Contractor

As an independent contractor, it is essential to understand the process of responding to IRS audits and inquiries. While the thought of being audited may be intimidating, with proper knowledge and preparation, you can navigate through the process smoothly. In this subchapter, we will discuss important strategies and guidelines to help you effectively respond to IRS audits and inquiries.

First and foremost, it is crucial to keep meticulous records. Maintaining accurate and organized documentation of your income, expenses, and deductions will not only simplify your tax filing process but will also serve as evidence in case of an audit. Ensure that you have receipts, invoices, bank statements, and any other relevant documents readily accessible.

In the event of an audit or inquiry, it is advisable to seek professional help. Hiring a qualified tax professional who specializes in tax planning for self-employed individuals can provide you with invaluable guidance throughout the process. They can help you understand the IRS guidelines for tax planning as a contractor and assist you in preparing your responses to IRS inquiries.

When responding to an audit, it is important to remain calm and cooperative. Promptly respond to any requests for information or documentation from the IRS. If you are unable to meet a deadline, communicate with the IRS and request an extension. Cooperating with the IRS demonstrates your willingness to resolve any issues and can positively influence the outcome of the audit.

During an audit, the IRS may question certain deductions you have claimed. It is important to be prepared to provide supporting documentation for each deduction. Familiarize yourself with the tax deductions for independent contractors and ensure you have all the necessary evidence to substantiate your claims. This may include receipts, contracts, mileage logs, or any other relevant documentation.

Lastly, it is crucial to understand your rights as a taxpayer. The IRS has guidelines and protocols in place to ensure fair treatment during audits and inquiries. Familiarize yourself with these rights to protect yourself and ensure a smooth process.

In conclusion, responding to IRS audits and inquiries as an independent contractor requires careful preparation, organization, and professional guidance. By keeping meticulous records, seeking professional help, remaining cooperative, providing supporting documentation, and understanding your rights, you can effectively navigate through the process and achieve a favorable outcome. Remember, being proactive and well-informed is key to successful tax planning as a contractor.

Avoiding Common IRS Red Flags for Contractors

As an independent contractor, managing your taxes can be a challenging task. The Internal Revenue Service (IRS) has specific guidelines and regulations that must be followed to ensure compliance and avoid any unwanted attention. This subchapter will provide valuable insights into avoiding common IRS red flags for contractors, helping you navigate the complex world of tax planning and deductions.

One of the most critical aspects of tax planning for independent contractors is properly documenting and categorizing your expenses. The IRS closely scrutinizes deductions claimed by contractors, making it essential to maintain accurate records. Keep detailed records of all business-related expenses, such as supplies, equipment, and travel expenses. Ensure that these expenses are legitimate and necessary for your business operations.

Another common red flag for contractors is the misclassification of workers. The IRS distinguishes between employees and independent contractors, and misclassifying workers can lead to penalties and audits. It is crucial to understand the criteria used to determine whether a worker is an employee or an independent contractor. Familiarize yourself with the IRS guidelines to ensure proper classification and avoid any potential issues.

Additionally, accurately reporting your income is vital to avoid any discrepancies that may raise red flags. Contractors often receive income from multiple clients, making it essential to keep track of all payments received. Ensure that all income is reported accurately on your tax return, and keep documentation to support these figures.

Another area that often triggers IRS scrutiny is the home office deduction. While this deduction can be beneficial for contractors who work from home, it is crucial to meet specific criteria set by the IRS. Understand the guidelines for claiming the home office deduction and ensure that your workspace meets the requirements to avoid any potential red flags.

Lastly, staying informed about changes in tax laws and regulations is crucial for contractors. The IRS frequently updates its guidelines, and being aware of these changes will help you remain compliant. Consider consulting with a tax professional who specializes in working with independent contractors to ensure that you are up to date with the latest regulations and taking full advantage of available deductions.

In conclusion, navigating the IRS as an independent contractor requires careful tax planning and adherence to the IRS guidelines. By avoiding common red flags such as improper documentation, misclassification of workers, inaccurate income reporting, and misunderstanding home office deductions, you can minimize the risk of audits and penalties. Stay informed, keep meticulous records, and seek professional advice when necessary to maximize tax deductions and ensure compliance with IRS regulations.

Staying Compliant with IRS Guidelines and Regulations

As an independent contractor, it is crucial to understand and adhere to the guidelines and regulations set forth by the Internal Revenue Service (IRS). Failing to comply with these rules can result in penalties, fines, and unnecessary stress. In this subchapter, we will explore the key aspects of staying compliant with IRS guidelines and regulations, providing you with the knowledge and strategies necessary for successful tax planning.

Tax deductions for independent contractors play a significant role in reducing your overall tax liability. However, it is essential to understand which deductions are allowed and how to properly document them. This subchapter will provide you with a comprehensive list of eligible deductions, including business expenses, travel and entertainment expenses, home office deductions, and more. Additionally, we will discuss the importance of maintaining accurate records and receipts to support your deductions, ensuring you are prepared in case of an audit.

Tax planning for self-employed individuals is another critical aspect of staying compliant with IRS guidelines. By creating a tax plan that aligns with your business goals and financial situation, you can optimize your tax strategy and minimize your tax liability. This subchapter will explore various tax planning strategies, such as income deferral, retirement contributions, and estimated tax payments. We will also address the benefits of consulting with a tax professional to ensure your plan is tailored to your specific needs.

Understanding IRS guidelines for tax planning as a contractor is vital to avoid any unintentional errors or omissions on your tax return. This subchapter will provide an overview of the IRS guidelines concerning income reporting, self-employment taxes, and estimated tax payments. We will discuss the importance of accurately classifying your income and staying up to date with the latest tax laws and regulations. By staying informed and proactive, you can mitigate the risk of IRS audits and penalties.

In conclusion, staying compliant with IRS guidelines and regulations is crucial for independent contractors. By familiarizing yourself with tax deductions, implementing effective tax planning strategies, and understanding IRS guidelines, you can ensure compliance and minimize your tax liability. This subchapter aims to equip you with the knowledge and tools necessary to navigate the complex world of taxes successfully. Remember, consulting with a tax professional is always recommended to ensure you are making informed decisions and maximizing your tax benefits as an independent contractor.

Chapter 5: Advanced Tax Planning Strategies for Independent Contractors

Incorporating Tax-Free Fringe Benefits into Compensation Packages

As an independent contractor, it is crucial to maximize your tax deductions and plan your taxes effectively. The Internal Revenue Service (IRS) provides guidelines for tax planning specifically tailored to contractors, enabling you to take advantage of various benefits and deductions. One powerful strategy to consider is incorporating tax-free fringe benefits into your compensation packages.

Tax-free fringe benefits are non-cash benefits that you can offer to your employees or yourself as an independent contractor without incurring additional tax liabilities. By including these benefits in your compensation packages, you not only attract and retain top talent but also reduce your taxable income, resulting in significant tax savings.

One popular tax-free fringe benefit is health insurance coverage. As an independent contractor, you may be eligible for deducting premiums paid for health insurance, including coverage for yourself, your spouse, and dependents. By providing health insurance benefits to your employees, you can also claim deductions for their premiums, further reducing your overall tax liability.

Additionally, you can offer retirement plans such as Individual Retirement Accounts (IRAs) or Simplified Employee Pension (SEP) plans. Contributions made to these plans are tax-deductible, allowing you to save for retirement while reducing your taxable income. Offering retirement benefits not only benefits you as a contractor but also enhances your appeal to potential employees.

Another tax-free fringe benefit to consider is educational assistance. You can provide your employees or yourself with tax-free educational assistance of up to $5,250 per year. This benefit covers expenses related to courses, tuition, fees, and books, enabling you or your employees to enhance their skills while enjoying tax savings.

Furthermore, transportation benefits, such as providing parking or transit passes to employees, can also be offered as tax-free fringe benefits. These benefits not only encourage eco-friendly commuting but also offer tax advantages by reducing your taxable income.

When incorporating tax-free fringe benefits into compensation packages, it is essential to comply with IRS guidelines. Ensure that you document these benefits properly and meet all the necessary requirements to avoid any potential penalties or audits.

In conclusion, by incorporating tax-free fringe benefits into your compensation packages, you can enjoy significant tax savings as an independent contractor. Health insurance coverage, retirement plans, educational assistance, and transportation benefits are just a few examples of the tax-free fringe benefits you can offer. Familiarize yourself with IRS guidelines and consult with a tax professional to ensure you are utilizing these benefits effectively. By doing so, you can enhance your overall compensation package, attract top talent, and optimize your tax planning strategies as a contractor.

Utilizing Section 179 and Bonus Depreciation for Asset Purchases

As an independent contractor, it is crucial to understand and take advantage of the various tax planning strategies available to optimize your financial situation. Two key provisions that can significantly benefit contractors when it comes to asset purchases are Section 179 and Bonus Depreciation. By leveraging these provisions, you can maximize tax deductions and minimize your tax liability.

Section 179 of the Internal Revenue Code allows you to deduct the full purchase price of qualifying equipment and software in the year it is placed into service. This deduction is available for both new and used assets, making it an attractive option for contractors looking to invest in their business. However, there are limits to the amount you can deduct under Section 179, which can vary from year to year. It's important to stay updated on the current limits to ensure you can take full advantage of this provision.

Bonus Depreciation, on the other hand, allows you to deduct a percentage of the cost of qualifying assets in the year they are placed into service. This provision is particularly beneficial for contractors as it allows for an additional deduction on top of regular depreciation. The percentage of bonus depreciation can also vary from year to year, so staying informed about the current rates is crucial for effective tax planning.

By combining Section 179 and Bonus Depreciation, contractors can significantly reduce their taxable income and increase their cash flow. This can be particularly advantageous for those who rely on expensive equipment or technology in their line of work, as they can deduct a substantial portion of these costs upfront.

43

To ensure you are eligible for these deductions, it is important to understand the IRS guidelines for tax planning as a contractor. Keeping detailed records of your asset purchases, maintaining receipts, and accurately tracking the date each asset is placed into service are all crucial steps to substantiate your deductions. Additionally, consulting with a tax professional who specializes in tax planning for self-employed individuals can provide valuable insights and help you navigate the complexities of the tax code.

In conclusion, Section 179 and Bonus Depreciation are powerful tools that independent contractors can utilize to maximize their tax deductions and minimize their tax liability. By staying informed about the current limits and rates, maintaining accurate records, and seeking professional advice, contractors can effectively plan their taxes and optimize their financial situation.

Implementing Tax Deferral Strategies for Long-Term Gain

As an independent contractor, understanding and implementing tax deferral strategies can significantly impact your long-term financial success. By deferring taxes, you can effectively manage your cash flow and potentially reduce your overall tax liability. In this subchapter, we will explore some key tax deferral strategies that can benefit contractors like you.

One important strategy for tax deferral is contributing to retirement accounts. By contributing to a traditional IRA or a solo 401(k) plan, you can defer taxes on the funds you contribute until you withdraw them in retirement. This not only helps you save for the future but also allows you to lower your taxable income in the present.

Another effective tax deferral strategy is utilizing a health savings account (HSA). If you have a high-deductible health insurance plan, you can contribute pre-tax dollars to an HSA, which can be used to pay for qualified medical expenses. By doing so, you can lower your taxable income while setting aside funds for future healthcare costs.

Additionally, consider exploring the benefits of a 1031 exchange if you own real estate. This strategy allows you to defer capital gains taxes by reinvesting the proceeds from the sale of one property into a like-kind property. By deferring taxes in this manner, you can continue to grow your real estate portfolio without immediate tax consequences.

Furthermore, it is crucial to keep meticulous records of all business-related expenses. By maximizing your deductions, you can effectively reduce your taxable income. Common deductions for independent contractors include office supplies, travel expenses, professional development courses, and home office expenses. Familiarize yourself with the IRS guidelines for eligible deductions to ensure you are taking advantage of every opportunity to reduce your tax burden.

Tax planning is an ongoing process, and it is essential to stay informed about changes in tax laws and regulations that may impact independent contractors. Consider consulting with a tax professional who specializes in working with self-employed individuals to ensure you are implementing the most effective tax deferral strategies for your unique situation.

In conclusion, implementing tax deferral strategies can provide independent contractors with long-term financial benefits. By contributing to retirement accounts, utilizing health savings accounts, exploring 1031 exchanges, and maximizing deductions, you can effectively manage your tax liability and optimize your cash flow. Stay informed and seek professional advice to navigate the intricacies of tax planning as a contractor.

Exploring Tax Planning Opportunities through Charitable Contributions

One often overlooked but highly effective tax planning strategy for independent contractors is leveraging charitable contributions. Not only can charitable giving make a positive impact on society, but it can also provide contractors with valuable tax deductions and potential savings.

Tax deductions for independent contractors are crucial for minimizing tax liabilities and maximizing profits. By understanding the intricacies of tax planning for self-employed individuals, contractors can strategically utilize charitable contributions to their advantage.

The Internal Revenue Service (IRS) provides guidelines for tax planning as a contractor, including rules and regulations related to charitable deductions. Contractors can take advantage of these guidelines to optimize their tax planning strategies and reduce their taxable income.

Charitable contributions made to qualified organizations can be deducted from a contractor's taxable income, effectively lowering their overall tax liability. However, it is essential to ensure that the charitable organization meets the IRS's criteria for deductibility. Contractors should research and verify the nonprofit's eligibility status before making any contributions.

Besides the immediate tax deductions, contractors can also explore long-term tax planning opportunities through charitable contributions. Establishing a donor-advised fund (DAF) or a private foundation allows contractors to contribute assets, such as stocks or real estate, and receive an immediate tax deduction while retaining control over the donated funds. This approach allows for continued growth and charitable giving over time.

Contractors can also consider donating appreciated assets, such as stocks or mutual funds, instead of cash. By doing so, contractors can avoid paying capital gains tax on the appreciated value of the asset while still receiving a charitable deduction for the full market value of the asset.

Another tax planning opportunity for independent contractors is through volunteering. While contractors cannot deduct the value of their time, they can deduct certain expenses incurred while volunteering for qualified charitable organizations. These expenses may include travel, meals, and supplies directly related to the volunteer work.

In summary, exploring tax planning opportunities through charitable contributions can provide independent contractors with significant benefits. By understanding the IRS guidelines for tax planning as a contractor, contractors can strategically leverage charitable deductions to reduce their tax liabilities while making a positive impact on society. Considering options such as donor-advised funds, donating appreciated assets, and deducting volunteering expenses can further enhance the tax planning strategy for contractors.

Understanding State and Local Tax Obligations for Contractors

As an independent contractor, it is crucial to have a comprehensive understanding of your tax obligations at both the state and local levels. Failing to comply with these obligations can lead to penalties, audits, and unnecessary stress. In this subchapter, we will delve into the intricacies of state and local tax obligations for contractors, providing you with the knowledge and tools necessary to navigate this complex landscape.

One of the first steps in understanding your state and local tax obligations is determining whether you have a nexus in a particular state. A nexus refers to a significant presence that triggers tax liability in that state. This presence can be established through various factors such as physical location, sales revenue, or the number of days worked in a particular state. Understanding your nexus is crucial as it determines whether you are required to register, file, and pay taxes in that state.

Once you have determined your nexus, it is essential to familiarize yourself with the specific tax obligations imposed by each state. States have different tax structures and regulations, including income taxes, sales taxes, and payroll taxes. Some states might have additional taxes, such as gross receipts taxes or franchise taxes. Researching and understanding these obligations will help you stay compliant and avoid any surprises when tax season arrives.

Local tax obligations also play a significant role in your overall tax planning strategy. Many cities and municipalities impose their own taxes, such as local income taxes or business license taxes. It is crucial to be aware of these local tax requirements and factor them into your financial planning.

Navigating state and local tax obligations as a contractor can be challenging, but with proper planning and organization, it can be manageable. Keeping detailed records of your income, expenses, and business activities will not only help you with tax compliance but also provide valuable documentation in case of an audit.

In conclusion, understanding your state and local tax obligations as a contractor is essential for effective tax planning. By familiarizing yourself with the rules and regulations imposed by each state and municipality, you can ensure compliance and avoid any unnecessary penalties. Stay organized, keep accurate records, and consult with a tax professional when needed to maximize your tax deductions and minimize your tax liability.

Adjusting Tax Planning Strategies for Changing Economic and Legal Landscapes

In today's ever-changing economic and legal landscapes, it is crucial for independent contractors to stay updated on the latest tax planning strategies. As an independent contractor, understanding how to navigate the Internal Revenue Service (IRS) guidelines and adapt your tax planning can make a significant difference in maximizing your deductions and minimizing your tax liability.

Tax deductions for independent contractors play a vital role in reducing taxable income. By strategically utilizing the available deductions, contractors can lower their tax burden and increase their bottom line. However, it is essential to stay informed about the ever-evolving tax laws and regulations to ensure compliance and take advantage of all eligible deductions.

One key aspect of tax planning for self-employed individuals is keeping detailed records of all business-related expenses. This includes maintaining receipts, invoices, and other documentation to substantiate your deductions. By organizing and tracking expenses such as office supplies, equipment, travel, and client meetings, you can accurately claim deductions and avoid any potential red flags during an IRS audit.

To effectively adjust tax planning strategies, independent contractors must also be aware of the IRS guidelines specifically tailored to their unique circumstances. The IRS provides comprehensive guidance on tax planning for contractors, covering topics such as estimated tax payments, self-employment tax, and retirement planning options. Understanding these guidelines can help contractors make informed decisions about estimated tax payments throughout the year, ensuring they are meeting their tax obligations while avoiding penalties and interest.

Furthermore, contractors should pay attention to changes in the economic landscape that can impact their tax planning strategies. Economic shifts, such as changes in tax rates, new deductions or credits, or alterations to business expenses, can significantly affect your tax liability. Staying informed about these changes and seeking professional advice can help you proactively adjust your tax planning strategies to align with the current economic climate.

In conclusion, independent contractors must proactively adjust their tax planning strategies to adapt to changing economic and legal landscapes. By familiarizing themselves with the IRS guidelines, tracking business expenses diligently, and staying informed about economic changes, contractors can maximize their tax deductions, minimize their tax liability, and ensure compliance with tax laws. Navigating the IRS requires continuous learning and adaptation, but with the right knowledge and strategic planning, independent contractors can confidently manage their tax obligations and achieve financial success.

Chapter 6: Conclusion and Action Steps for Successful Tax Planning

Recap of Key Concepts and Strategies Covered in the Book

Throughout the book "Navigating the IRS: Tax Planning Strategies for Independent Contractors," we have delved deep into the intricacies of tax planning for self-employed individuals. As contractors, understanding the nuances of tax deductions, planning, and IRS guidelines is crucial for maximizing your earnings and minimizing your tax liability. In this subchapter, we will recap the key concepts and strategies covered in the book to provide you with a comprehensive overview.

One of the fundamental topics discussed in the book is tax deductions for independent contractors. We highlighted various deductible expenses that contractors often overlook, such as home office expenses, travel and transportation costs, professional development and training expenses, and health insurance premiums. By taking advantage of these deductions, contractors can significantly reduce their taxable income and ultimately pay less in taxes.

Tax planning for self-employed individuals was another important theme explored in the book. We emphasized the significance of creating a tax plan tailored to your specific circumstances. This involves estimating your income, tracking expenses, and regularly reviewing your financial statements to ensure compliance with IRS guidelines. By implementing effective tax planning strategies, contractors can better manage their cash flow, avoid surprises come tax season, and potentially access tax credits and incentives.

Throughout the book, we provided detailed insights into the IRS guidelines for tax planning as a contractor. We emphasized the importance of maintaining accurate records and documentation to substantiate your deductions, as well as the need to stay up to date with the ever-changing tax laws and regulations. We also discussed the benefits of working with tax professionals who specialize in assisting independent contractors, as they can guide you through the complexities of tax planning and ensure compliance with IRS guidelines.

In conclusion, "Navigating the IRS: Tax Planning Strategies for Independent Contractors" has equipped you with the knowledge and tools necessary to navigate the intricacies of tax planning as a contractor. By understanding tax deductions, implementing effective tax planning strategies, and adhering to IRS guidelines, you can optimize your financial well-being and achieve greater success in your independent contracting career. Remember, maximizing your earnings and minimizing your tax liability is not only legal but also essential for your long-term financial success.

Developing a Personalized Tax Planning Roadmap as an Independent Contractor

As an independent contractor, navigating the complex world of taxes can be a daunting task. However, with proper planning and understanding of the IRS guidelines, you can develop a personalized tax planning roadmap that maximizes your deductions and optimizes your tax savings. This chapter will guide you through the essential steps to help you create a solid tax strategy tailored to your specific needs.

Tax deductions for independent contractors play a crucial role in reducing your taxable income. By identifying and claiming all eligible deductions, you can significantly lower your tax liability. This subchapter will provide an in-depth exploration of the various tax deductions available to independent contractors, such as home office expenses, business-related travel and meals, health insurance premiums, and retirement contributions. We will also discuss the importance of keeping detailed records and receipts to substantiate your deductions and ensure compliance with IRS regulations.

Tax planning for self-employed individuals goes beyond mere deduction identification. It involves proactive strategies to minimize your tax burden and optimize your financial well-being. This subchapter will explore advanced tax planning techniques, such as income shifting, estimated tax payments, and retirement planning. By implementing these strategies effectively, you can reduce your tax liability while simultaneously planning for your future financial security.

Understanding IRS guidelines for tax planning as a contractor is crucial to ensure compliance and avoid potential penalties. This subchapter will provide a comprehensive overview of the key IRS guidelines that independent contractors must adhere to. We will discuss topics such as self-employment taxes, estimated tax payments, and record-keeping requirements. By staying informed about the latest IRS regulations, you can confidently navigate the tax landscape and avoid any unpleasant surprises during an audit.

In conclusion, developing a personalized tax planning roadmap is essential for independent contractors seeking to minimize their tax liability and maximize their financial well-being. By understanding the available tax deductions, implementing advanced tax planning strategies, and adhering to IRS guidelines, you can effectively manage your taxes and achieve long-term financial success. This subchapter will equip you with the necessary knowledge and tools to take control of your tax planning and ensure compliance with the ever-evolving tax laws.

Resources for Further Assistance and Expert Advice

Being an independent contractor comes with numerous advantages, but it also means taking on the responsibility of managing your own taxes. Navigating the complex world of tax planning can be daunting, but with the right resources and expert advice, you can ensure that you are maximizing your tax deductions while staying in compliance with IRS guidelines.

1. IRS Website: The Internal Revenue Service (IRS) website is an invaluable resource for independent contractors. It provides comprehensive information on tax laws, regulations, and guidelines specifically tailored to self-employed individuals. From understanding deductible expenses to estimating quarterly tax payments, the IRS website offers a wealth of information to help you navigate the tax planning process.

2. Tax Professionals: Hiring a tax professional who specializes in working with independent contractors can be a game-changer. They have in-depth knowledge of the tax laws and regulations that apply specifically to contractors, ensuring that you take advantage of every available deduction while avoiding costly mistakes. A tax professional can also provide personalized advice and guidance tailored to your unique situation.

3. Online Communities and Forums: Joining online communities and forums for independent contractors can be an excellent way to connect with others in your field and gain insights into tax planning strategies.

Platforms such as Reddit, LinkedIn groups, and specialized contractor forums offer opportunities to ask questions, share experiences, and learn from others who have faced similar challenges.

4. Small Business Development Centers (SBDCs): SBDCs, typically affiliated with universities or local government entities, offer a range of resources and services for small business owners and independent contractors. They often provide workshops, seminars, and one-on-one counseling sessions that cover various aspects of running a business, including tax planning. Contact your local SBDC to find out about the specific programs available in your area.

5. Professional Associations: Many professional associations provide resources and support to independent contractors in specific industries. These associations often have tax planning resources tailored to their members' needs and may offer webinars, articles, and networking opportunities related to tax planning. Consider joining an association related to your niche to access these valuable resources.

Remember, tax planning is an ongoing process, and it is essential to stay informed about changes in tax laws and regulations that may affect your business. By utilizing the resources mentioned above and seeking expert advice when needed, you can confidently navigate the IRS guidelines and maximize your tax deductions as an independent contractor.

Taking Action: Implementing Effective Tax Planning Techniques

Tax planning is a crucial aspect of financial management for independent contractors. By utilizing effective tax planning techniques, contractors can minimize their tax liabilities and maximize their after-tax income. In this subchapter, we will explore various strategies and guidelines provided by the IRS to help contractors navigate the complex world of tax planning.

One of the key areas to focus on when it comes to tax planning for independent contractors is maximizing tax deductions. As a contractor, you are entitled to deduct various business expenses from your income, resulting in a lower taxable income. These deductions can include expenses such as office supplies, equipment, travel, and professional development. By keeping detailed records of these expenses and understanding the IRS guidelines, you can ensure that you are taking advantage of all available deductions.

Additionally, self-employed individuals must consider the importance of tax planning throughout the year, rather than just during tax season. By implementing effective tax planning techniques year-round, contractors can better manage their cash flow and avoid any surprises when it comes time to file their tax returns. This includes setting aside a portion of your income for estimated quarterly tax payments to avoid any penalties or interest charges.

Understanding the IRS guidelines for tax planning as a contractor is essential for compliance and avoiding any potential audits. The IRS provides specific rules and regulations for self-employed individuals, and it is crucial to stay up to date with these guidelines to ensure that you are meeting all of your tax obligations. This includes properly categorizing income and expenses, keeping accurate records, and understanding the requirements for reporting and filing taxes as an independent contractor.

Implementing effective tax planning techniques also involves seeking professional help when needed. As the tax landscape can be complex, contractors may benefit from consulting with a tax professional who specializes in working with self-employed individuals. These professionals can provide valuable advice and guidance tailored to your specific situation, ensuring that you are taking advantage of all available tax-saving opportunities while remaining compliant with IRS regulations.

In conclusion, taking action and implementing effective tax planning techniques is essential for independent contractors to optimize their tax situation. By maximizing deductions, staying informed about IRS guidelines, and seeking professional assistance when needed, contractors can navigate the IRS with confidence and ensure that their tax planning strategies are working in their favor.

Monitoring and Adjusting Tax Planning Strategies for Ongoing Success

As an independent contractor, understanding and implementing effective tax planning strategies is crucial to optimizing your financial success. However, tax laws and regulations are constantly evolving, making it essential to monitor and adjust your strategies to ensure ongoing compliance and maximize your tax deductions. In this subchapter, we will explore the importance of monitoring and adjusting tax planning strategies for contractors and provide practical guidance on how to navigate the IRS guidelines.

Tax deductions for independent contractors play a significant role in reducing your tax liability and increasing your overall income. However, it's crucial to stay updated on the ever-changing tax laws to take advantage of all available deductions. Regularly reviewing your expenses and understanding which deductions are applicable to your business can help you identify areas where you can save money. This may include deductions for home office expenses, business-related travel, equipment purchases, or professional development courses. By monitoring these deductions and adjusting your strategies accordingly, you can ensure you are taking full advantage of the tax benefits available to you.

Tax planning for self-employed individuals requires a proactive approach. It's important to regularly review your financial records, income, and expenses to determine if any adjustments are needed. By tracking your income and expenses throughout the year, you can identify potential tax liabilities and make necessary adjustments to avoid any surprises during tax season. This may involve adjusting your estimated tax payments or implementing additional tax-saving strategies, such as contributing to a retirement plan or setting up a health savings account.

The IRS guidelines for tax planning as a contractor can be complex and overwhelming. However, by staying informed and seeking professional advice when necessary, you can ensure compliance and maximize your tax benefits. Regularly reviewing IRS publications, attending tax seminars, or consulting with a qualified tax professional can provide valuable insights into current regulations and help you make informed decisions about your tax planning strategies.

In conclusion, monitoring and adjusting tax planning strategies is crucial for ongoing success as an independent contractor. By staying updated on tax deductions, regularly reviewing your financial records, and complying with IRS guidelines, you can ensure you are optimizing your tax benefits and minimizing your tax liability. Remember, seeking professional advice is always a wise choice to navigate the intricate tax landscape effectively.

www.ingramcontent.com/pod-product-compliance
Lightning Source LLC
Chambersburg PA
CBHW040324010626
45792CB00024B/2122